# Stripped

Also by Liezel Graham

POETRY

*A Counting of Love*

# Stripped

Liezel Graham

Quiet Rebel Press

for **Noah Daniel**

for you i lay down my darkness

# Contents

Acknowledgements

# Preface

This collection of poems and micro-poems is as much about (my) becoming, as it is about (my) unbecoming.

My words are simple and some of these poems are not much more than a single sentence, but it is my deepest hope that through them, you might know that your story matters, and that you have always been enough.

Walk with me?

Let me tell you of the profound and astonishing wonder of choosing a new life, every day.

every woman who heals herself
heals her children's
children.

— break the chains

hope, is such a tender gift to give.

— it looks so beautiful on you

what if you should find yourself hiding
right here inside my words?

then you should eat them.

fill your belly with the poetry from my bones.

then you will know
that you are not
the only one.

— my words are yours

the words that you write on your own skin
are the hardest to erase.

— edit boldly | rewrite yourself

sometimes
it is not who you are,
so much as who you are not.

— do not become the one who hurt you

do not use the stones that were thrown at you
as ammunition.

you can be a strong and peaceful place.

if you choose to be.

— choose (your) peace

perhaps if i spoke plainly of my winter

you would have no need to search desperately
for your spring

if i could speak of the taste of the red dust
in my throat

and if you would listen

then perhaps i might be the rain
in your dry season, too

soft and soothing

until life blooms for you once again
in all your barren places.

— i have been where you are

i want to fall back

into
myself

crawl through my bones
until i find them green again

so that i might whisper a different story
to my cells.

— one more chance

you cannot eat someone else's pain
to fill the hunger in your bones.

— we who are hungry, make ourselves needed

it is no small thing | to sing in the storm.

— courage

come,
the world said.

everything about you is wrong.

let me show you how to fit in—how to belong.

i am sorry,
i whispered, but

i am too busy healing myself to be afraid of you anymore.

— when it finally rains

being loved, and
        being used for love.

both taste the same
to a hungry heart.

— a hungry heart is a dangerous thing

all of these holes in the walls of my heart

because you could not give me
what you did not possess.

but look!
i have filled them up with silence,

watered them with beauty, and

flowers have grown where once there was nothing.

— i am no longer hungry for what you could not give

when you leave
do not take the one who hurt you

with you.

— let it stop with you

there are many ways to live your life, and some are braver than others.

and a whole lot of my life ago, a man once said to me,

you have to be more selfish.
stop giving yourself away so much.

as if this were the answer to everything.

but it's not.

and for a little while i tried to live like that.
like him.

narrow and small.
but it didn't work for me, and

i began to see that all that i am
is all that i have.

and surely, all the pieces of me were made to be given away?

the smooth pieces that shine like love in the moonlight?
i have given them all to you. and you hold them now
in your hands and in your heart, and you will always
remember me.

even when i am gone.

the jagged piece that cracked when a bullet flew right across
the kitchen, and everything inside me shattered?
that piece is still here
with me.
i have not found anyone with pain in the same shape as mine
to give it to.
yet.

but i am sure that i will one day.
they all find a home
eventually.

some are very old.
some are very frayed.
some need to be dusted first, but i find hearts for all of them.
every single one has a home.
somewhere.

and i have noticed that nobody cares about dust
if i have given them with love.

and i always wrap them well, with pieces of my own heart
stuck on top—a bit of wild hope.

and then there are also these shiny bits that sparkle
like happiness on a sandy beach.
but not.
and what came next, i still don't have a name for, and
that day was all it could be, but i have given it away now.
and you.
and i have healed myself.
i don't need these pieces anymore.
or you.
and what you took from me, has grown and i have given it to the
others—quietly, so that the world cannot see the thing that we
have to carry.

until we are ready.

even in this, there is a gift.

and i have given many pieces to strangers in the street,
and sometimes even outside holy places, in the pouring rain.

and they are little gifts to tired mothers who are hungry to be
seen, and the old man bent down towards his death, whose hope
had all run away.

and i hold them in my hands—these tiny scraps of me—and
i say,

*here! please take this! i have more than i need.*

and then i smile, and i show them the sun in the sky, and also my
heart, and sometimes a miracle happens right there in front of my
eyes.

but not always.
no.
not always, and there are times that i am not wanted.
or my heart.

and for a little while it stings, but only until i turn the corner and
walk straight into the next heart. and this is how i live.

big and open—the blue sky on a warm summer's day.

and i give.
and i give.
and i give myself away

until one day, right at the end, there will be nothing left of me.

i hope.

and all over my life, there will be pieces of me growing
here, and there, and maybe even everywhere.

and this is how you live.
and this is how you love.

crazy big and madly bold.
and it takes courage.
don't be fooled.
but do it!

do it if you can, because none of it is meant to leave with you,
so don't even try to hold onto all the love that you have.

and you have so much that if you scratched your skin
it would come flowing out.

like water.

so, please
don't hold onto it.

trust me.

it really only works when you give it all away.

— how to live your life in pieces

how many layers did they wallpaper onto your skin?

undoing is gentle work.
be patient with your
heart.

— this is how you heal

mercy is a blanket | with which we all need to be covered.

— i have been naked too

if the silver birch
when autumn whispers

can undress herself

discarding all that no longer has life

laying
bare

the starkness of her bones
without a thought for any opinion

then so shall i.

— stripped

a heart can splinter under the weight of a memory.

i choose to bleed hope
instead of pain.

— when war breaks out inside my head

i am a house of many rooms.

through these passageways,
quiet and dusty,

sunlight drips liquid gold, and

it falls almost everywhere
that i go, and

how i love to drink hot Assam tea,

malty on my tongue, and
comforting

as i walk through these spaces,

gently touching all the things i had almost forgotten about.

but
not
yet.

it is comforting to find old friends.

you.
and you.
and yes, even you.

we must stay in touch,
i say to the past.

a smile.
a nod.

let's not forget about each other,
yet.

it would be good to sit and talk
for a bit,
every now and then.
but there are also corners and dark spaces
where the light does not
reach, and

doors that are locked.

i stand before them with the key.

still, i cannot enter.

i cannot enter, and i know that i must.

there is work to be done within.
but not yet.

not yet.

— there are places that i cannot go yet

this tender heart of mine.

i fight a war every day
just to keep it soft.

— guard your heart

i caught every stone you threw at me, and
built myself this fortress.

i feel so safe
enclosed
by all these walls.

how i wish that they weren't so high.

— hidden

when i was twelve
i learnt that i could

love
someone
and fear them

at the same time.

that a father could write words
on the inside of his daughter's eyes

that would blur her vision forever.

a wall of graffiti by another's hand, despite

a holy whitewash, and

i have tried.

and i have learnt that if your eyes are illuminated
with the light born from knowing
that you are safe, that

you will not understand this language
scrawled on hidden walls.

this tongue of violent words
spray-painted onto
virgin territory
and

i learnt to search

for
voices

who know how to wallpaper the inside of my brain, and

this is work that never ends.

with each new layer the message fades
a little more.

just a little more.

until i almost believe that i once was enough.

— graffiti

i am seeking out all the places
where my voice
was stolen

leaving poems filled with flowers in exchange.

— on healing from the past

this work of living
as water

allowing it to trickle
liquid
hope
from my belly

even when my bones are dry

it is a brave life.

— on living as water

and then there was the time

a whole lifetime
really

if i am honest

and honesty opens the door
they say

when i allowed my heart to be carried away by thieves
who faded silently into the dark

because i was not enough for me

because the voice inside my bones
found me
wanting

and i believed the lies

and all i have ever wanted
was to be
enough

such a hungry word
enough

and i have scraped portions of my heart
onto the plates
of others, and

by feeding them
i have tried to fill my own belly

a feeble attempt at peace

but i am not enough to ease hunger

i am not fish, or even a tiny piece of bread
i know this now

and i am learning to trust, that
everything that i am
is all that you have ever wanted

enough
such a full word

and that i can call off the search, for

love
and
hope
and
self-respect

and all the other light-filled things that i have searched for

in the thorns
and
in the words
and
in the arms

of others

there is nothing tame about this
it is a wild unravelling
of whom i am

all the way back to the beginning of me.

— unravel

i will not apologise for seeking beauty
in barren places.

— (i have always been) hungry for more

i am not soft and beautiful

fluent in the language of women
who know how to act, and
how to speak, and

how to be
pliable
and
round
and
tame

this i have always known, and

i carry it fiercely

it scares you
i know

i am thorn and metal
shaped by war, and

somewhere between nine, and
all the other years that formed my skin

i learnt how to keep my edges sharp and wild

unrestrainable

this is where i hide.

— on being wild

my heart is such a tender
fertile place.

i won't let just anybody walk through it.

— refuge

this extravagant gift of life
wildly beating
just a little while longer.

what grace is this?

— song of the grateful

you do not always have to be Martha,

furiously
working
your
way
into
peace.

you are allowed to be Mary.

Mary,
who ate rest in the midst of chaos.

— a reminder to all the women within me

i once knew a woman
round and lush and nurturing

who fought a war with her body

believing that by becoming
less

she would become
more

until she was hollow

but still the numbers
did not equate
with peace

they never do

do they?

— scale

a man once told me,
if only you were smaller i could love you, more

perhaps, if there was less of you.

and if only i had seen
just
how
thin
he was
in all the wrong places, and

just
how
little
there was to him
and to his love,

perhaps, i would not have lost so much
of me.

but i was young, and
i was soft in all the right places

so, i took all of his words
and i wrapped my thighs
and my hips, and my breasts, and my soul

until i was completely hidden, and

it was the sixth day, and

it
was
still dark.

and later, others came and said,
you are too tall i cannot see myself when i am next to you.

and can't you see that there has to be less of you,

and more of me,

for the Bible tells you so.

and
you
must
obey.

and they grew thicker.
the layers.
until they were walls.

and all i knew was how to live smaller
but never small enough.

until one night, i heard my body weeping.
a year ago, or forty.

or perhaps, it was right at the beginning
when blame fell like blood on the first woman's
shoulders, and i said

enough!

i will not carry this
anymore, and

i will throw down this weight.
it does not have my name on it anymore.

and in the dark i ran my hands

over my head, and my arms, and my legs, and my toes.

and i felt all the things that were stuck there.
all of their hatred.
and all of
mine
too.

stuck deep inside all of my softness.

and i felt my belly.
this ripe, round roof
over the holy space within me that grew a whole child.

and you dare say that i am not enough?

and i said thank you to my heart for beating,
and beating,
and beating,
and for never giving up on me

despite my trying.

and i whispered love to my lungs for the breath,
always the breath that i now find in sacred stretches, and
in other holy places in the back of my eyes
where they could never
ever see.

and i felt my breasts
full of the beauty that gave life to a child, and
they are not here just for your amusement.

and neither am i.

and i have had enough of this war.

and i ran my fingers over my skin, and my bones.
and my past, and my hopes.

and i unhooked everything there.

every word.
everyone, and
every single thing that i never invited in.

until all that was left
was me.

here in the light.
it is good.

— woman | unhooked

tell me, what of these hips of mine?

they are a lush fullness.
beauty untethered.
a quiet rebellion.

i am a woman at peace in her own skin.

— have you ever seen such an untamed peace?

some days are about saying no, and
letting go of people

who have seen the tender parts of your heart
and
still
they
walk
through
the soft new grass
with a bag of thorns to sow, and

mercy is a gentle rain, and

forgiveness

might bring life, but

remember your own heart first, and

how long it took
for flowers to bloom
from the cracks in the dirt.

— your heart deserves more

when will you let go of the idea that
carrying the anger
and
the bitterness of those you love, is

how you love?

you can sit with them for a while.
                        the ones you love.

even every day, if you must, and
you can help them unwrap all that hurt, but

afterwards

put it back where it belongs, and

if it is still wanted,
leave it with its owner.

it
is
not
yours
to carry home,

even though it might feel as if you must.

sometimes, love is about leaving things behind and

knowing when to go back for more.

if
you
must.

— when anger is wanted | leave

do not be afraid of being cracked wide open.
you are bleeding healing onto others.

— how to bleed healing

i am naked.
stripped bare
from learning how to love every part of me.

— undo

i want to take off my skin
slice deep into the past
cut through my fears

right
into
my
sin

and all the things that i should leave behind
but won't

i want to dive into the green of the water
where peace is silent
and deep, and

perhaps, forgiveness lies at the bottom
soft and without breath

but i don't
not yet

and i wonder how much regret weighs, and

how long it will take before i can no longer carry it.

— shackles

if the child deep within your skin
                    is weeping
sit with her in sorrow

rub kindness into her wounds
                    sing love over all her fears

this
is how you will both heal.

— pour grace over yourself

there are nights
and also, sometimes days
where she finds me lying in darkness, and
we go back

back, as far as she wants to go

and i let her decide where we will stop
and linger for a bit

i have learnt to trust her
with this most important thing

sometimes, we walk through my father's garden
he is there, and
so am i

the sun is hot on my young skin, and
the cicadas shrill in the shimmering of the late afternoon, but

we are happy and content

i hold this in my cupped hands
it is treasure

i ask him the secret to growing strawberries
sweeter than syrup, and yes
he could create
beauty from
nothing

but sometimes, she whispers softly in my ear

ask him the hard questions, like

how-will-i-know-when-the-corn-is-ready-to-be-picked
if its fullness is hidden, and

please show me how to read the clouds that gather over the
Karoo landscape

and then he tells me all the secret things that a gardener
needs to know, and it is rain falling from a broken sky
flooding the dry earth, or

perhaps it is my heart
that is finally
wet

but sometimes, she makes me stop where words are acid
my skin burns, my

heart
melts
like
lead
over an open flame

and then, when i have cooled into a different shape
all i can do is stand there, my hand
on her shoulder

and i tell her that it's all right

it's all going to be ok, and
you are going to be
fine

just you wait and see, and

please, let all of these words fall off your skin
please, don't let them cling to you, and
when the tears come

let them

let them water you, and

let them fall where they will, and
it is never too late to let them come, and
just you wait

you will see that one day

life

will find you in the light, and
all of this will still be there, but faded

with no more power left
to hurt

and when we come back
we hug, and

we say goodbye for a little while

this is hard work

too hard for every day, and
she leaves me
quietly

i get up
and i read stories to my son
who looks at me with so much love
that i can hardly believe my life

and somewhere
the corn is yellow and ripe, and i hear her laugh.

— when she takes me back

did you think that you could undo

all
the
hurt

by becoming just like them?

hatred
for hatred.

anger
for anger.

no, darling, no!

you have to scrape their whitewash right off your skin.

unlearn the songs that they forced you to sing

and
only
then

will flowers fall from your tongue like water, and

you will be free.

— return to yourself

and still, you bloom wild courage
in a thousand little ways
despite your winter.

aren't you a miracle?

— on living brave

she said,
do you know that i have been hungry for so long
from birth, i think

that i have fed all the soft parts of me to hundreds
maybe more, and still, it is not enough
when the light breaks over me
like glass, and

i am never enough, and
only one of us leaves with a full belly, and
it is never me

it is never me who knows what it feels like to be enough
to be just right
not too much and not too little

and i don't know how to get all my pieces back

my heart needs them back because the holes are so big now
the wind blows right through them, and sometimes
late at night when all those people
are walking through my head
with their hungry bellies
and their dirty feet

i can't sleep for the sound of the weeping
that howls right through me

and perhaps it is not them
perhaps, it is me
i don't know anymore

and all i could say was, i know.
me too.

— Elizabeth

54

you can fashion anything
out of pain

even a new life
if your heart is soft enough.

— forgive

this man makes me feel so alive, she said,
and he is everything that i have ever wanted, but still

he is not enough.
still i need more.

and i don't know what it is.
and why do i have this thirst in the middle of my heart
and how do i fill it, if not

with love?

and i looked at my friend with the father-shaped hole
right in the middle of her heart,
and i asked her gently,

because some words are spiky when they leave your mouth, and
they need to be unwrapped
with soft hands,

do you know the difference between honey and water?

do you know that there are men
who will pour you cups of honey and oh, it will be so sweet
on your tongue, and you will feel all the holes in your heart
fill up with the golden stickiness of it, and

for a little while

if you are very lucky,
and if you learn this lesson quickly,

you might believe that honey is liquid love.

it is not.

it will never be enough,

because honey will never quench your thirst.

you have to wait for a man who is running water,
pure and full of life.
a man who will pour himself out, and
into your cupped hands, and
over your head, dripping
down into your bones,
filling up that thirst
in the middle of
your heart.

flooding it with the one thing that always gives life, and

only then will you know that there is a difference between words
that fall sweetly from the tongue, and
the men that use them, and

words that can make a second-hand thirst go away, and
they are not the same thing.

honey and water.

but there is more, and

what you really should know, is this

it is not for a man to heal your heart, and
some men will try if their hearts are big enough for two, and
if they love you enough, but

it is not fair to expect a man to lie down in a hole made by
another, so that you can walk across him
to the other side, and

you have to find your own way out of pain, and
when you finally swim to the edge of that, and

crawl your way out through the mud, then

and only then,
will you know the difference between honey and water.


and you will know which men bring life in their hands, and which
men don't.

and you will never confuse them again.

and then you will teach your daughter how to sniff the air
for the scent of rain, and you will show her how to walk
away
from things that do not flow over her thirst with life, and

she will learn how to swim to the edge, and
she will grow strong from climbing out of holes
made by others, and

she will stand on the thing that wanted to drown her,

but couldn't.

and water will run down her limbs, and it will drip from her skin
onto the dry ground until everything under her feet
blooms green.

this, will be your gift to her.

— honey and water | for Elizabeth

do not be afraid
to take up more space
when the light has finally found you.

— grow

look at me, she said.

all these walls are crumbling around me, and

every woman that i am
is suddenly
afraid

but every morning i hear the blackbird
singing in the old sycamore
across the road

a tree that is naked all winter
until the light comes and loves her again

and then all at once
she too
isn't naked anymore

and i know what that feels like, and

i know that he sings for me

the blackbird

only for me, and i think he knows that walls tumbling down
and
limbs greening up towards heaven, and

a woman planting healing all over her own naked feet
all take their own time.

miracles will not be rushed.

— new

send your roots down deep into the silence of the earth.

when the rain falls hard on your tender leaves
let it be so.

turn your face up towards the sun, and
let the light
find you.

— on how to survive | advice from an oak tree

who was i before i could hold my head up,
look the moon in the eye,
and smile?

i can hardly remember.

i have walked barefoot through quiet streams for so long now
and my hands are too full to carry old words with me, and

did you know that truth can be unlearned,
even and especially when,

it has been glued onto you
by other hands.

it can be removed.

all is not lost or carved into your bones.

remember when they said that you were too much for them?

that you should grow smaller

so that you could fit into the palm of their hands?

listen to this.
listen to me.

too narrow, and
too small,

they
were
never
enough

for you.

and sometimes, hearts that have been broken
will demand that you shrink
so that they can carry the weight of their own lack.
again, listen to me.

it is not yours to carry, and
it is not you that must grow smaller.

let this truth breathe life into your fear, and

now you can wrap these words around your hips and show them
off to the whole world.

you are a cup running over onto everyone who sees your heart.

listen to me!

there has never been a time
that you have not been
enough.

— why are you shrinking under the weight of their lack?

did you think that

all
this
undoing

would be easy, that

you
would
escape
unnoticed

by those who have drawn square lines

all
the
way
around
your softness, and

have you ever seen an apology
fall
from
a single leaf
on the wild cherry tree
when she abandons her winter
in
wild
white
wonder.

— apologies are not for trees | or for you | or for me

it is ok to be soft during a war | surrender to yourself.

— be gentle with yourself

the woman said, i woke up wise one morning a long time ago
after i walked into a man's heart and got lost.

and again today, i have done the same thing, and

i don't know why i forget this lesson so often, and

every now and then when the child inside me is searching for
anything and anyone to clear the fog from the windows
when she can't see out of her heart, she searches for someone
else to see in.

if only for a little while.

and i have always been the kind of woman who walks
straight into people, and
i search their eyes, and
their smiles, and
somehow

their hearts are open doors to me.

but not every open door has a welcome mat on the floor, and
why can't i remember this?

it would hurt so much less.

to some i have only been skin and form.
a swell of hip, and rise of breast

but nothing more.

and i have searched for a price tag that i might place on my heart

deep within their words, and adjectives don't fill me up
anymore, and

some people don't use them often enough, you know—their
words, and others again use too many, and also too much
of you, and

let me tell you about these people.
if you walk into them with love in your hands,
you will get lost in the cave of their hearts,
searching for a way out of them,

stumbling around in the dark,.
leaving pieces of yourself on their walls, but also

i know now, never to go back to search for myself.
or my heart.

and it's ok, because cave people won't keep your heart, and
some of them won't even notice that it's there, and

if you really want to find yourself again, you need to wait for the
darkest night, when the Milky Way opens herself up before you
like a shy lover.

then you have to climb the highest mountain that you can find.

do this in the dark.

you will skin your knees and your bones might break.
there will be pain and even loss, but you will find yourself there.

in the dark.

yes, you will.

and you will be so much more than the weight of their hot words
on your skin.

and so much more than mouth, and breast, and naked limbs.

and all your lost pieces will return to you, and even your heart
will flutter right out of his cave.

i have seen this with my own eyes, and when the light
pours herself out over the horizon, your heart
will find you
again.

and when it is all over, and

dry your eyes now.
some things are not worth your tears.
especially if they were only ever dressed up as love, and

when the work of placing your heart back where she belongs
is done, you must stop for a little while.

rest.

talk to the child inside your head.
tell her that a woman does not need a string of pearls
or a ring,

or the warm honeyed words of a man
to hang around
her neck.

she only needs the stars, and the light, and the warmth of her
own breath, to know that she is everything and more.

enough.

— when the woman learned the lesson once again

all the things that were taken from my hands

have found their way back to me
as words.

— loss, has made me fertile

he tells me how men are made

first, by breaking everything gentle that ever had a chance to
grow towards the light

as if a man was never grown
below a woman's
heart

and then, by searing
the wounds with
white-hot
shame

there are things that he still cannot say

his words own him

sometimes at night, he allows himself to feel everything
that will not leave
his mouth

it lives there

large and silent

this is how men are made by other men

later, in the half-light of a dying day i tell my son

who still has sunshine and softness
living inside his mouth
that all his words are

naked

when they climb up his throat

they are not to be dressed up
before they fall like stars
from his tongue, and

they all belong
to him

this, is how his heart will walk out of his mouth one day

i am building a man, too.

— how to build a man from the inside out

just as i was swallowing
the impossible blue
of the morning
sky

the thing that knows my name

crawled
darkly
onto my lap, and

stayed

and for a moment i was lost in every war
that ever
fought
me

but you

you with your three words
strung
on a sling

your heart in your hands

a pebble that slays.

— i love you

it happened one morning as the light from today
fell on yesterday's scars, and

i remembered

the sand, the blue of the sea, and the sun burning my shoulders,

and i ate the fire, and
was that all that was sacrificed that day?

i was there with you, or were you there with me?
i forget some things.

a mercy.

i wanted to say

no.

but words get lost on the wind sometimes
don't they, and

i want to undo that day.

take a scalpel to my skin and cut

all the way through, until

you disappear.

until i can free myself from all that you turned out to be.

but i can't.

some things cannot be unravelled,
or unlived.

i have tried, but

have you heard how a heart splinters
when things are taken from half-open hands?

i have had enough of eating a dead season's pain.

see here, where i have drawn a line in the sand?

i have stepped over you now,
back into my own life, and

this, is where you stay.

— on leaving dead things behind

did you know
that
hope
can fall like a leaf in october, slowly

dancing its way to death

as
it
is
let go of.

and then, be

reimagined
rebelieved
rehoped

in the spring?

— a metamorphosis of hope

throw it open.

that thing coiled up tight inside.
that dark question with sharp teeth.

that answer that you have dressed up in bright colours, but
its name is loss, and also

you know that this-is-not-for-you.

throw it open and let the light fall on it.

let the wind find all the hidden things that are dressed up
        as what they are not.
                and what they will never be.
open it all up.

i dare you.

your eyes want to see what you have known all along.

— your heart has always known

if you have wandered through your life for a while, and
perhaps you have outlived your old skin, and curious
things have happened to your lines, and your
colours have started to bleed, then

let me tell you something true!

a day will come, unexpected in its light,

when you will have to fight, and raise your new voice in a victory
song so that you will be heard, and

although they may have walked through your life
as a friend does,

they
will
need
proof
of this new change within you.

this metamorphosis unauthorised by their hand, and

it will hurt.

all change does,
at least for a little while.

but here you are, all grown up!
and
you have grown in,

into your new skin, now
stretched taut
                    over all that was once fear-thin, and
your roots have grown strong.
and all of this new hunger needs good soil, and so

you must search until you find the thing
that fills your bones
with joy.

and you have worried about the leaves
that have withered in places, and
about the mess
all over your
feet.

there is no need to cry over things that are dying,

or people who leave.

death
makes
room
for more, and

see how you are already greening all over, but

they will find this uncomfortable,

find you
uncomfortable
to shelter underneath.

at once preferring the sparseness
                    of whom you once were, and

not this new, verdant canopy
obscuring their view
of whom they
want you
to be
again

your rawness will offend them.

it will disturb their sense of right,

and
you
will
be wrong.

so, fight if you must.

if you have to prove the worth of your new life,
then fight.

but also know this,

there are others out there,
many others, and

one day,
on a sunny afternoon
unexpected in its warm light,
they will stumble upon your presence, and

they will come and they will linger longingly in your shade

and there,

right there where the others found nothing left of worth,

they will find shelter
and rest.

— when you have changed

it is not so much that
i cannot
breathe
behind
doors
that are closed by another's hand, and

how i always need
every
window
open
wide
to the smell of rain as earth yields to water.

no.

it is that i have
slowly
become
the weather
that you were told to seek shelter from.

— the shape of rain

the light wakes me early.

the night that was only three-hundred-and-eighty broken minutes
long, has left me tender and unready for the life of all these new
hours that stretch ahead of me.

and i have pulled myself back from sleep three times in the name
of all that is holy, so that i can steal blood
from my sleeping son's finger, and

is there enough glucose for him to wake again, in the morning?

not too much
and not too little.
the porridge must be just right, said the baby bear.

but last night, it wasn't.

and there were numbers so low that they wrapped my heart up
in cold fear.

and there was apple juice and an oat biscuit in the dark hours.

sit up my boy,
and drink.

and with eyes closed,
he hears my voice, and he drinks

just like a long time ago, and somehow i still keep him alive.
and isn't this a miracle, i whisper to myself.

and 'just right', is what the magazines say that i must be.

not too hot—how dare she?
not too cold—hasn't she let herself go?

and there is a woman on every page.
and there is a woman in every word.

shiny
unlined
and untested women.

and i hear them tell me how to erase the gentle rise and fall
of my body's topography, and also

they say that i should feel shame at the contour lines that caress
the outer landscape of my womb, and

over there, someone with teeth as white as revelation,
tells me how to pretend that my hips have never held a heartbeat,

and that my breasts have never flowed with life, and

this is how you must shine if you want it all, she says
with a smile.

and who doesn't want that?

but *today* has a new name.
it is *brave*, and

somehow, i have kept a child alive in the dark.
can you believe that?

i ask all the pretty girls on all the perfect pages, and

finally, i am tired enough to say

please, don't tell me how to be beautiful.
just don't.

i have no room in my life for your imperfections.

i watch as the fresh, unlived morning climbs in through my
bedroom window.

it falls softly on my tired skin.
it makes everything
beautiful.

especially me.

and i hear all the pretty women, and

the woman that i tried to be
a long time ago.

and every man who told me how to be just-right,
how to be everything that they had ever dreamed of.

listen!

i hear them weeping as i fold my body

down
down
down

towards my roots, and all that i can hear is their hunger,

and it is no longer mine.

somehow, i have kept a child alive in the dark.

can you believe that?

— please, don't tell me how to be beautiful

i am reconstructing me | there is a savage beauty in this work.

— your approval is not required

the early morning air is cold on my skin.

the trees are pulling on their red coats again, and

are they showing off, or
are they hiding?

i don't know.

but there is a new dragon in my mouth, and

look! we are breathing fire, mom!
my son says.

i nod quietly.
i know the flames well, but
i don't always know how to tame them, and

sometimes, they climb up my throat
speaking a language i thought i had left behind.

this fire in my words.

another life.
another everything, but
still i am there.

a part of me has never left that wild country.

just beneath my skin
i still am.

i do not like who i am there, but
a part of me is planted there

still.

in the mossy undergrowth we find an acorn.
the squirrels must have overlooked this one, or
perhaps it was left here just for us.

he holds it in his boy-hand that is already bigger than it was last
week, and

eleven years ago.

all of him becoming something new.
something more.

and me trying to undo.
always,

scraping.
scraping.
scraping.

hoping, that eventually less of me will show.

it is a seed, he says.
his eyes examine mine for what to believe.

i shake my head.
no, i say.
it is not just a seed.
it is another chance.
there is an entire forest lying in your hand.
it is all there inside.

if you care for it gently,
you will grow
again.

— there is a forest within you | another chance

strip yourself bare
so that you can find the place where the wildflowers grow.

— find yourself (again)

one starry night, the woman took a walk inside herself
to all the quiet places that she loved to go, and
there under the warm Karoo sun, she
played barefoot again.

unworried about snow and ice, and other cold things,
her young hands could tease the dry soil
for fragments of glass
again.

blue,

if you must know and hidden deep inside the earth.

just like me.

and one day i shall be an archaeologist, and i shall dig for things
in the dirt

beautiful things.

just like me.

and i shall have rooms full of books, and they will all be mine,
and nobody will ever take them away, and

i shall walk all over the skin of the world, and i shall see pyramids
and other broken things, and we shall see each other, and

we shall smile at each other,

all the broken things and i.

and i shall never have to prove that i really do know things.
and they are all wrong about me.

and perhaps then, i shall finally belong.

and i wonder what that feels like?
to fit snugly in a place, and inside a life.

as if your shape was made to belong just there,
in that very place.

but some don't,
do they?

belong?

some people are not made to fit into round holes, because they
have sharp edges, and sharp corners, and

the loveliest things hide there, but not everybody can see that.

and not everybody knows how to look for treasure
in sharp-cornered people, and it takes a long time for a square
heart to know that is ok to not be round.

and i have been scratching in the dirt for years searching for
hope, and life, and other green things, and i have grown soft
with love for myself.

and even now, i still look for pieces of discarded peace, and
other broken things, in places where others only see dirt.

and this is my gift

to see the loveliness in a man's skin, and
to hear Africa in his deep voice as our children swim together
here,

far from home.

but not everybody sees him.
and i see the fragile hope in the eyes of a woman

who ran from bullets, and who crossed deserts, with babies
in her arms, and

then still the oceans too?

and what did she know about water so deep and so fierce,
other than that, it was safer than the hearts that she ran from.

but not everybody sees her, either.

and i look for smiles, and people who walk straight into you
with mouths that bow up to the light, and eyes
that sparkle like glass
in the sun.

these are the things that i search for now, and when i find them,
i turn them over and over in my hands, until i am warm inside.

and it doesn't take long before my hunger is satisfied, because
there is enough beauty everywhere to fill every starving belly.

and then later
i hide them deep in a corner.

and oh!

i wish you could see all the beauty that i have hidden here
on this side of my walls.

i have finally found the place where all my edges belong.

— on finding my place

it can take a lifetime

to
fit
into
your
skin.

keep stretching.

— change

i am afraid of people who refuse to change their minds.

i am a life made of seasons.

change, is in my blood.

— if you find a new truth, turn your back on the old one

have they come back
to haunt you
again?

all the women that you once were?

do you also
wake up to the way you once walked the earth

sitting there,

darkly

on the edge of your bed

whilst the whole world is quietly sleeping?

as if there has only ever been peace beneath the night sky, and
in your bones, and

you know that
that,
is not true.

don't you?

but also,
you know better now, and

you exit a room differently now,
to the way that you once did
before?

so gentle you are now,
and strong.

your eyes always searching for the light, and
look at you!

so fierce you are in your fight to never be the same

as you once-upon-a-time were, and

yes,

you know so much better now,

don't you?

perhaps, it is time that you let them all go.

the women that you once were,

but aren't anymore?

leave them on the edge of your darkness, and
walk on brave girl.

walk on.

— they will try to come back | walk on

still i bloom.

roses tumbling from my wounds.
a wild offering of hope.

— i will not give up

the poet fears the loss of words to rearrange on paper, and

there are many places in the heart a drought can happen, but

last night i told my son a story
before sleep claimed him
from me,

and he laughed,
and laughed.

his mouth a happy moon in a dark night, and

this morning, my words carried the sun on their shoulders
as they left my mouth to call him back, and
he heard and smiled in his sleep.

this is how far they can travel
when they do not need my
permission.

the poet fears the loss of words that will obey her on paper, but

see how many quiet ones slip out when she is not looking.
but they will not be shaped into poems
where they do not want to live.

no.

some words are made to fall all over sleep-soft skin.

they are made entirely of love.

— my words are always making poems

put yesterday down
outside the front door, and

leave tomorrow by the window

the light will shine on it soon enough

hush now
this is today's song

a simple refrain

speak to yourself with love

rub kindness into your skin, and

look!

wildflowers are waiting to bloom from all your broken places.

— forgive yourself

you

be the softness that you need
the kindness
that you did not receive

be all the things that will sustain you
until your hands overflow
with healing.

— rub oil into your scars

do you still have that dream?

the one that you have been dressing, and
undressing since you were little?

breathing in the joy
of knowing that
this,

this beautiful thing belongs to you, and
only you, but

then
they made
you build a fence
all the way around the thing that made you happy.

kept you out
and away
from
it.

your face pressed right up against the magic,
but
not
close
enough. and

did they say,
who do you think you are
and
that will never happen. and

did they say,
you are not like them.
      you are like us. and
people like us don't dream, and

you think that you are so much better than us,
don't you?

but you are not, because

you
are
one
of
us.

do you remember it now?

i thought you might.

let me tell you this,
the voices are the same no matter who you are, or
who you were

in-the-beginning.

and that fence might be overgrown by now.

mine was.

and it might be higher than you thought it was
when you still believed
in dreams.

it happens.
don't worry about it.

don't worry about thorns,
and weeds,
and other strangling things that can be cut back,
ripped out,
and

broken down.

that will be the easy part.

what i want to know is this,

and this is really the most important thing

do you still hear their voices?

well, do you?

because that is where the lie started, and
that is where the lie
must end.

so,
turn
your
back
dreamer, yes

you must do this if you are still searching for that thing
that made you feel alive, and

it will need some care, and
a little bit of love.

but it will live.
if you want it to.

so, this is what you do.
you listen for another voice, and
it is quiet
and
it is soft,
so, listen carefully.

it says i-believe-in-you things, like

what a wonderful idea,
and
i know that you can do this,
and
you are just the right one for this dream.

let me tell you something else

sometimes, there is a lot of noise when fences come down,
and when dreams go up, up, up into the sky again.

don't worry about this.

it will die down.
and
you will grow up.
and
you will grow out towards your new horizon.
and
you will find your way again.

because the thing that gave you joy,
is still waiting for you, and

if you are brave, and
if you are certain
that this is
what you
want,

then one day,
sooner than you think,
you will walk straight into yourself again.

— the thing that gave you joy is (still) waiting

.

i am filled with silence
and flowers.

i am a fragrant peace.

— i am not who you told me i am

the only way to heal

is to undo the way that you were put together
by others.

— break yourself wide open

you are allowed to mourn everything
that you did not receive.

but do not live there permanently.

grief, is both a jailer and a gift.

— on mourning that which was never given

every now and then,
you should take off all your fears
and expose them to the light.

— let the light in

at the end of a monday that has sharp claws, and much later than
a small body should still be awake, he asks me,

why do you call me Danny?

there is fire in his eyes.
his body is taut with challenge, and
something else that i cannot give a name to,

but i know that it needs to be set free by my hands.

and we are all tired from pretending that today was easy.
there are deep rivers that need to be crossed carefully
with bare feet.

it is easy to slip and fall when your heart is tired
and there is fire in your mouth, and

when a mother falls, she takes her child with her.

i hand him the little bit that is left of me, and
i am always in awe at how many little bits i still have left, and
how they never seem to run out,

even when i shake the bag and it sounds completely empty.

i tell him,

it is just a nickname my boy.
something a little different to your real name.
sometimes people use nicknames for someone they love.

but i think of all the names that were painted onto me.
all the names that didn't see me.
all the names that forced a different life onto me, and
how i fought to stand up under their weight.

in the half-light of my son's bedroom i see the same fight in his boy-eyes that are now the same green as mine.

how did that happen?

there was a time that they were something else—blue, like the ocean, but he has grown out of that, and he is stretching into a different shape now.

growing into his skin.

my name is Daniel and nothing else!

his words fly at me like ravens.
they are black and angry.

but i catch them, and i hold them in my hands
until they stop biting.
until they soften.

and i nod my head gently, and i say,

yes, your name is Daniel.

that is who you are.

you are nobody else.

— a lesson in names

the way that the earth yields herself
in hunger
to the tenderness of the rain.

i have to look away from all this love.

— rapture

around the corner,
in the street where i live,

a rose, the colour of the evening sky
as the sun makes love to the light
         just once more before she leaves for the night,

spills boldly over the safety of the fence that holds her in.

she could have stayed small
and
hidden, but

she didn't.

throwing
herself wildly
at narrow-eyed commuters walking to the bus stop, and

children, on their way home from school,
boisterous in their fresh freedom, their eyes
on the weekend, and

happy dogs who run past this
perfect
offering
of pink,
but who don't care much for roses, and

tired mothers
who did once care for pretty things, and
         for making love,

but their eyes now chase small children

and all their lost dreams. and

perhaps, for them, roses are from a different life.
from before. and

perhaps, it will find them again.

one day.

and then
there is me.
when i walk past that fence, my eyes wide open in wonder
at her glorious
unrepentant
beauty,

and how she dares
to seduce me shamelessly into joy,

petals perfectly pink,

right here in the middle of the day

where everyone can see
if only they looked.

and her.

not caring for a single moment
whether i fall in love
with her,

or not.

but i do.

oh, how i do!

— how to be seduced by life

do not think it a small thing
to be
alive
today

go and squander it

      foolishly if you must

on the sun
on the rain
on the trees


but whatever you do
do not curl inward
to die
before the music stops playing

it will do so soon enough

live sumptuously

feast on the sound of the wind
susurrating through the trees, and

soak up the rich death of autumn leaves until you glow
with a life lived bravely, and it is time to sigh your farewell, but
not until

not until.

— on how to live in the shadow of death

this wild wonder
of choosing a new life

every day.

— what can i say about such a gift?

if you are fortunate, you might get to walk through the valley
of the shadow of death.

perhaps you might walk right through it, and
            not everybody does.

it is not a given, but it is a gift.

and nobody knows who will unwrap this favour with their
unwilling hands, but if you do

then walk all the way in—eyes wide open—with fear sometimes,
yes, but also in wonder, and with your hands lifted
            up
in search of the light, and then

after a lot of hope has passed, you might walk right out the other
side.

straight into a second chance.

and i did.

and things were never quite the same inside of me again.

second chances do that to a life.

and for the rest of my days, even until today, i am learning how
to plant fresh healing right outside my own front door,

every single day, until

the air smells like a fistful of yellow freesias, or hot pink
geraniums in the afternoon sun—until the fragrance clings to
me—my hands, my skin, my hair, and until all my words smell
like hope.

i have discovered quite by chance, or maybe not, that i can paint
the inside of my life with colours that shout at the dark.

and they sing in wild abandon when everyone around me
is silent with the weight of their fear, but not me.
and all the hours that were never promised to me

or to you,

now fill up my hands and spill right onto my feet, and they water
the earth everywhere i walk.

and sometimes in the late afternoon light, i dance to the music
inside my head, but

you won't hear it though.
it only plays for me.

and sometimes they laugh, but i don't care.

i have taken off my old skin now.
i am finally naked with hope.

and now i can feel—really feel—the wet, salty air from the ocean
on my limbs—like a stolen afternoon of making love. and i now
wear perfume in the hollow of my neck, and
behind my ears,

even if, but especially when, i am just cleaning my house.

everything is worth celebrating.

and in the shop i search for oranges that smell like the southern
tip of Africa.

or Spain.

and i fill my belly with rich, tender words that taste like Rumi and Hafiz—ancient Persia on my tongue, and i am brave enough now, to close doors on things that are not enough.

and a woman who can close a door, is a powerful peace.

and we who have had our travel plans disrupted and rerouted via the valley, we recognise each other.

even from far off.
even in our silence, we can tell who colours beyond the rules, and the walls, and all over the straight lines that keep us from seeing the light inside each other.

and detours and side roads are lonely places, it's true, but just like three a.m. and three miles in, the wilderness has a quiet peace that will fill you in the end.

if you let it.

and nothing inside you will ever be the same again, so

don't be afraid of unmarked roads, and maps ripped from your hands.

just don't.

fear has a name, and it is not yours.

there's a light within you, and a voice that knows which way to turn, and which way to go.

just trust.

second chances will do this to a life, and more.

i know.

one day, you will look up and the air will smell like flowers
and you will be soft in all the places that matter.

you will care, and also not, and

nothing will ever be the same again.

second chances will do this to a life.

— on second chances

i want to live my life
as brazen as the hyacinth on my kitchen windowsill

boldly
she has left behind the season where

all
she
knew
was darkness, and

knowing
that all that she is
is an evanescent breath

she gives herself unashamedly

to life.

— unashamed

you must look for its scent on the breeze.

be careful not to get distracted
by things that masquerade
as sustenance and

when you find it
soak it up through your skin

hope

drink wildly
hands cupped with desperation, and

then

draw a map from the well
to your thirst

so that you will never get lost again.

— how to drink water | when you finally find it

i want to eat beauty.

let it spill from my tongue
so that my words will have the fragrance of hope.

— i will make the world beautiful

how many fears have you faced?
how many giants have you slayed?

all the wars that have fought you,

have lost.

— you are not broken

i go to the shop for essentials.

eggs
bread
and bags
to line the kitchen bin.

but in the fruit aisle i am seduced by mangoes
from a far-off country, and

i fall in love

right there.

i have always given my heart away so easily.

i touch.
i pick up,
and i smell the ripe, red skin and
everything hidden that lies beneath.

i have never liked mangoes,
a woman says to me.
they are too messy,
and the juice
stains.

i nod quietly at her gospel, but

i go straight home to my kitchen
where nothing makes sense anymore
since a lifetime ago.

and here in the afternoon light,
i peel and i slice.
i cut away,
until

the flesh blooms ripe orange
in my hungry hands.
like the sun.

or courage.

and i eat the fragrant offering,
juice running down my chin
onto my shirt.

and i think to myself,

this will leave a mark that cannot be erased.

it tastes like freedom.

like everything that i have been searching for.

i feast hungrily.

— do you know what my freedom tastes like?

endings do not frighten me anymore.

every night the sun whispers farewell to the moon

only to rise again
with fresh
courage.

— and so do i

i became all the things | you told me | i could never be.

— you were wrong

a heart can be frozen soil
in the valley of winter, and

hope, might appear to be dead.

don't be afraid.

it is just sleeping.

the light will fall on it soon enough, and

snowdrops will birth themselves right in front of your eyes, and

you will breathe once again.

just wait for it.

— when your winter is too long

my words used to

wait
silently
at the door to my mouth

for permission to enter the world.

but look at them now!

they fly like birds
and
shooting stars
and
other holy things

that know just where to land.

— free

# Acknowledgements

My thanks to the editors of the following poetry journals in which some of the poems in this collection have previously appeared, albeit sometimes in a slightly different form, and with a different title.

*Anti-Heroin Chic,* for featuring, **Pour Grace Over Yourself.**

*Scarlet Leaf Review,* for featuring, **Undo.**

The poem, **On Living Brave**, was featured in the lyrics of the song, *Living Brave*, by singer and songwriter, Vicky Richardson of, *Keeper of Bees*. My gratitude goes to her, as well as to the band, *The Ocean Beneath*.

To hear my words sung as part of the lyrics in this song, is a real gift.

thank you for reading my words.
may you always know how to say your own name with love.

Made in the USA
Middletown, DE
04 August 2021

45294632R00087